Plants

Seeds

Patricia Whitehouse

Heinemann Library
Chicago, Illinois

www.heinemannraintree.com
Visit our website to find out more information about Heinemann-Raintree books.

To order:
☎ Phone 888-454-2279
🖥 Visit www.heinemannraintree.com to browse our catalog and order online.

©2009 Heinemann Library
an imprint of Capstone Global Library, LLC
Chicago, Illinois

Edited by Adrian Vigliano and Harriet Milles
Designed by Joanna Hinton Malivoire
Picture research by Elizabeth Alexander
Originated by Heinemann Library
Printed in China by South China Printing Company Ltd.

13 12 11 10 09
10 9 8 7 6 5 4 3 2

Library of Congress Cataloging-in-Publication Data
Whitehouse, Patricia, 1958-
    Seeds / Patricia Whitehouse.
        p. cm. — (Plants)
Includes index.
Summary: Introduces the physical traits, function, and uses of seeds.
    ISBN 978 1 4109 3477 2 (HC), 978 1 4109 3482 6 (Pbk.)
    1. Seeds--Juvenile literature. [1. Seeds.] I. Title. II. Plants (Des Plaines, Ill.)
    QK661 .W45 2002
    5581.4'67—dc21
                                    2001003651

Acknowledgments
The author and publishers are grateful to the following for permission to reproduce copyright material: Alamy pp. 4 (© Phil Degginger), 10, 23 (© Grant Heilman Photography), 12 (© allOver photography/ Alamy), 15 (© fstop20), 21 (© Richard Peters); iStockphoto p. 13 (© Klaas Lingbeek van Kranen); Photolibrary pp. 5 (SGM SGM), 7 (Stefano Stefani/Photodisc), 8 (Anthony Blake/Fresh Food Images), 9 (David Marsden/ Fresh Food Images), 11 (Cutting Ann/Botanica), 16, 23 (Oxford Scientific), 17 (Fritz Rauschenbach), 18 (Foodpix), 19 (Sandra Ivany/Botanica), 20 (Manfred Pfefferle/OSF); Shutterstock pp. **6 top left** (© TsR), **6 top right** (© Aleksandr Stennikov), **6 middle** (© Mau Horng), **6 middle right, 23** (© ultimathule), **6 bottom left** (© Elena Schweitzer), **6 bottom right** (© Yellowj), 14 (© LockStockBob).

Cover photograph of kiwano fruit slices reproduced with permission of Corbis/© bilderlounge. Back cover phototograph of a papaya reproduced with permission of Shutterstock (© Elena Schweitzer), and a coconut, iStockphoto (© Klaas Lingbeek van Kranen).

We would like to thank Louise Spilsbury for her invaluable help in the preparation of this book.

Every effort has been made to contact copyright holders of any material reproduced in this book. Any omissions will be rectified in subsequent printings if notice is given to the publisher.

All the Internet addresses (URLs) given in this book were valid at the time of going to press. However, due to the dynamic nature of the Internet, some addresses may have changed, or sites may have changed or ceased to exist since publication. While the author and Publishers regret any inconvenience this may cause readers, no responsibility for any such changes can be accepted by either the author or the Publishers.

Contents

Some words are shown in bold, **like this**. You can find them in the Glossary on page 23.

What Are the Parts of a Plant?

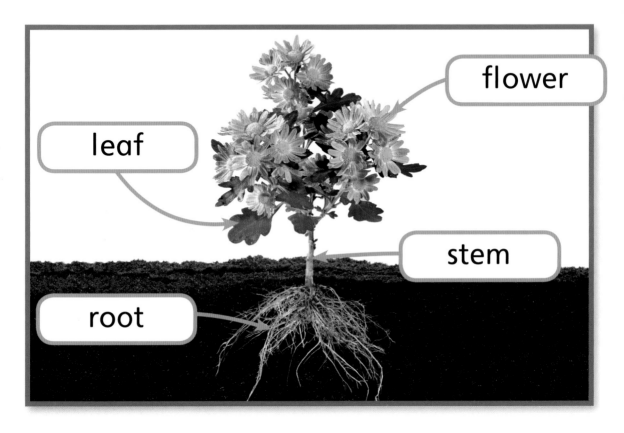

leaf

flower

stem

root

There are many different kinds of plants.

All plants are made up of the same parts.

seeds

Some plant parts grow above the ground in the light.

Most seeds grow inside parts of the plant.

What Are Seeds?

seeds

seeds

Seeds are part of a plant.

Some seeds grow inside soft **fruits**.

seed

Some seeds grow inside other kinds of fruits.

Nuts are seeds that grow inside hard, dry fruits.

Where Do Seeds Grow?

The flowers of a plant make seeds.

The seeds are part of the **fruit** of a plant.

The fruit grows bigger after the flower dies.

There are seeds inside this fruit.

Why Do Plants Have Seeds?

When seeds land in soil they make new plants.

The young plants are called **seedlings**.

Seedlings grow into plants.

The seedlings look just like the plant the seeds came from.

How Big Are Seeds?

Seeds come in many sizes.

These poppy seeds are tiny.

Some seeds are very big.

A coconut is a very big seed.

How Many Seeds Can a Plant Have?

A **fruit** may have just one seed.

An avocado has one big seed inside.

Some plants have lots of seeds.

A strawberry has many tiny seeds on the outside.

Why Are Seeds Different Shapes?

seed hooks

The shape of a seed helps it move to a place where it will grow.

Hooks help some seeds hold on to animal fur.

Some seeds are light and fluffy so they blow in the wind.

How Do People Use Seeds?

People use seeds for food.

We crush, squeeze, or pop open some fruits to eat the seeds inside.

We can put seeds in the ground.

Later the seeds will grow into new plants.

How Do Animals Use Seeds?

Animals use seeds for food, too.

Birds, squirrels, elephants, and monkeys eat seeds.

Some animals eat the seeds
right away.

Others bury their seeds to eat later.

Count and Record

This bar chart compares the number of seeds in different fruits.

Which fruit has the most seeds here?

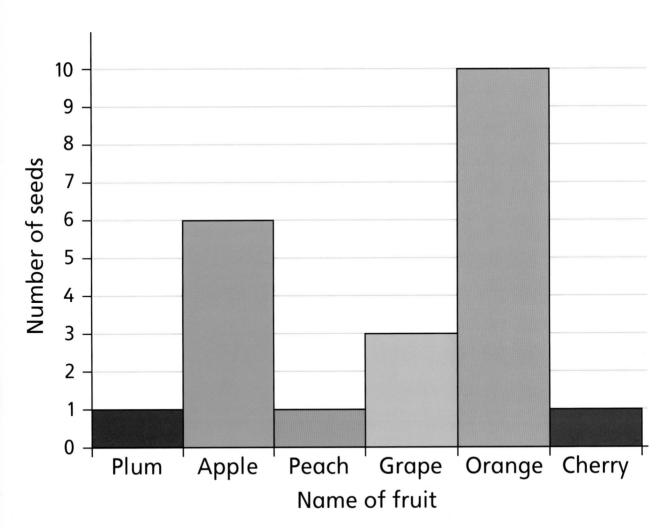

Glossary

 **fruit** the part of a plant where the seeds are

 **hook** the curved part of a seed that catches on to things

 **seedling** the new plant that has just come out of the ground

Index